Hide Your Eyes

The Rumi Poems

99% Press,
an imprint of Lasavia Publishing Ltd.
Auckland, New Zealand

www.lasaviapublishing.com

Copyright © Mike Johnson, 2020

Cover design by Jennifer Rackham, 2020

ISBN: 978-0-9951282-9-3

Mike Johnson

Hide Your Eyes

The Rumi Poems

Press

A rose's rarest essence
lives in the thorn

Rumi

Translation: Colman Barks, adapted.

No longer a stranger
you
listen all day
to these crazy love words

like a bee
you fill countless larders
with honey

though yours
is a long distance flight
from here

Rumi

Translation: Colman Barks, adapted.

where the truth lies

to cover the truth
with a handy lie
is to tell another kind of truth
about where truth lies

this is not as abstract as it sounds

lies hide
the most perfect truth of all
oh secret of my soul
oh Beloved of my heart
oh Guest of my flesh

make me whole
make me whole

lies show more than facts
which lack
that self-revealing fantasy touch
we bring to our lives
in the stories we tell each other
at bedtime
and in the morning

when we need to rise and shine
to pick up our narratives
where we left off
to get control where control
was lost

tears fly when this stuff
unfolds
when the lie and the truth lie down
together
and make up yet another good yarn
for the sake of the world
for the sake of our hearts

just to keep the narrative in line

give me a story we can recite
in all good faith
one we can chant
turn into ritual, an incantation
and bring us into our known world
with the least hassle

when the light goes out

Rumi's lament

Beloved!
there are times
when I am five miles high
enjoying the view
the clouds below
the void above
riding the bend of spacetime
waving my cowboy hat
and screaming whoopee

and other times
it's a fight to raise a smile
or find a rhyme
that doesn't show too clearly in the line

my name doesn't sound like me
anymore
I am not what I would be
I'm no dervish

I dance like a goose dreaming it's a swan
dive like a fish that's lost the sea

and fear the tears of the condemned
even as the drums roll
and the crowds whet their teeth
for the feast

I want more than a whore
I want it full bore
straight to the core
under the sheets of night

and a smorgasbord of stars
for our delight

let me see the Beloved smile

I want a theory of theories
that holds the big shout
with nothing left out
to wonder about
not just the mere cosmos
with its stupendous flights
dark planets and binary stars
but this stuff between my ears
hopes and tears
and all this thumpity-thump
of the heart

I'm no use if I can peer
behind the curtains of creation
and see the big bang in the making
hear the death rattle of the nation
yet can't track tears
from one side of my face
to the other

what's the use of being Rumi
if the left hand doesn't know
the right hand is its brother?

everybody's screaming
the deafening sound of lost love
but I'll sit with the quiet ones awhile
like you, Beloved
with your gentle face
and get a handle on it

if only
just for a moment
it would hold
in place

that greater frenzy

it's a pretty mess
what to say and do
and how we make up for it all
when the word gets about
and the girls gather
to admire your dress

from the face in the sky
you can't hide your eyes
or keep your quiet
when sharp-toothed demons
run riot
and Rumi gets left
to wrtite on the wall
after the party
and everybody who's anybody
has gone home
with what's left of their lives

perhaps She could never stand
to have her bodice ripped
by eager slaves
that we might behold

all that is in bold and
open form
lest we die of awe
with no one to pour
a little wine on our graves

for surely
we would die from that greater frenzy
before getting the chance
to clear away the tears
close the accounts
say goodbye to friends and fears
make a final stand
prepare ourselves for obliteration
covering the eyes of our children
with our naked hands

Upsidedown

hanging from your ankles
it's a world upsidedown
although it's hard to see the upside
of it
from this angle

people walk around on their hands
trees wave their roots in the air
while flowers bloom underground
and the moon grows
at the bottom of a lake

Rumi has witnessed this many times
without having to be drunk
under the influence of the moon
in the embrace of the Beloved
or bound to a stake

that's not all, my furry friends
because upsidedown means back to front
and inside out
as north turns south
and east and west swap beds

a staircase that goes only one way
words that run away from themselves
even as they walk backwards
out of your mouth

and mothers that butcher babies
even as they suckle them
and men that own the world
even as they gut it
and leaves that drift upwards
in a hawk wind
and lovers that fall out of graveyards
freshly born

lies that grow wings
to become butterflies
and a wind that skids backwards
over the sand
lifting the world with it

and that's not all comrades
of the dark, supplicants forlorn,
there's so much more
where that came from

cause and effect get
turned around
with effects turning into causes
and causes turning into
effects

arguments get stood on their heads
blatant stupidity presented as policy
hatred as righteousness
bigotry as bravery
blindness as blessing
love as perversion
art as crime
dusk as dawn
theirs as mine

so don't expect too much
as you hang
downside of this upsidedown
side, trending upside soon, no doubt
when the truth comes out
when all will be
put the right way up
for the last time
so help us
for the last time

Rumi's five-fingered exercises

don't set the bar too high
don't make the children cry
don't stone the crows that fly
don't make an honest man sly
don't raise that flag too high

don't make the children die
don't make your tears too shy
throw the bar into the sky
lift the children up on high
give the world a golden eye

Rumi's tribute to Dr Seuss

what you imagine you imagine
you imagine for real
everything else is a lie or a steal

everything else heads for the hills
everything else lives as it kills

don't be deceived by the girl at the pool
the shimmer and glimmer
as the lights grow dimmer
or the wise man in secret playing the fool
or the hypocrite in black copping a feel

what you imagine you imagine
you imagine for real

don't close your eyes when it's time to read
don't close your mouth when it's time to feed
don't shut your heart when it's time to bleed

what you imagine you imagine
you imagine for good
for bad or for worse or for love
of a deal

everything else is a maybe, perhaps
or a would
just something you heard
some gossipy rumours, a twisted word
randomly said
improperly read

what you imagine you imagine
changes the world
turns the stars around
turns love on its head
a tree into a high-flying bird

don't look the other way
when you're ready to play
what you imagine you imagine
won't go away

see-saw

did you see what you thought
you saw
or was the see-saw purely
for the playground
where children scream
and throw their hands into the air
and the Beloved walks the street unseen
and unrecognised
secret lover of her heart disguised

I saw what I thought I saw
because I couldn't see anything else
ever
what I thought I saw is all I see
for all eternity
and the poet was just so right
when he said that one thought
can fill immensity

what I thought I saw, I saw
and can't unsee
no matter how hard I try
or what's at stake

or how the heart
might hide the world
from the naked sky
or the naked sky might
hide the heart
from the world

it works whichever way you say it

all in hiding
from that invisible worm
that flies the night
and heedlessly buries itself
in the heart of the rose

Pan love

when Pan comes to town
he sleeps where he will
and enters dreams and bodies
and dream bodies
and body dreams
without so much as a please
or thank you

happy to be man or woman
as desire pleases
to shapeshift into the image
of the Beloved
(what's your pleasure?)
and to blow into the reeds
a melody so poignant
the heart melts
and the body opens
and the blood rises
and the rose turns
as Pan enters
and all the nymphs rejoice
to hear
the cries that go up to heaven
the ecstatic prayers

ascending to heaven
the prayers and pleas of helpless
throats
seeking the very tongue of heaven

leaving only the men and women
with their ordinary lives
on an ordinary morning
in the wreckage of their gardens
and their god-struck eyes

holding the baby

cats and monkeys

monkey swings along
the monkey bars
chittering and chattering
making up stories
never missing a beat
quicker than a flash
spreading the heat
opening the word
emptying the word
making love to the fair
flesh on fire, making love
to the very lineaments
of desire

no monkey this
no monkey moment either
swinging beyond
the teeth and the hair
wood and ash
the innocent and the liar

meanwhile
the yellow-eyed cat

parts the shadows
slips between the shadows
of the heat
bides its time
divides its time
purrs its time

nature breathes
the sweetest perfumes

and monkey never misses a beat

between the sheets

and you face the terror of knowing
that there is no in-between
knowing
and not knowing
between
love and death
between
the left and the right side
of the pumping heart

between seeing and seeing
and not being

there's
no scalpel sharp enough
to divide
love from love
nor wisdom enough
to bring them together
convincingly
for some sweet pillow talk

and as for your hands, well
they know where they've been
and you know it's best
when the left hand knows
what the right hand is doing
and they do it together
in mutual consent

there is no Goldilocks
moment
between high moon and
low sun
between melody and memory
between the penny and the penny arcade
between the moment of light
and the eternity of dark
between the devil
and the deep blue sea

between is a hard place to find
except between the sheets
somewhere between staying and fleeing

my god! the stars should be so wide
your heart a vessel of infinite depth
for your blood to race through

arteries of the earth and all her sister worlds
with you, you
mistress of all you behold
empress of all that ever was and will be
a tongue that arcs between the light
and the light

meanwhile, up dawn creeps
while your back is turned
shadows steal shadows out of the night
and you face the terror of knowing
there is no in-between
and no way of being
a goddess with a divided heart

except between the sheets

sacrifice

it was the touch that did it
the sacred touch
the touch that lights up
everything it touches

lightning-rod of the body
flesh of flesh, spark of spark
and the in-between of the flesh
where flesh parts
and love leaves its mark

feet that walk you over the earth
down the hall
through the archway and into the temple
hands held before you
beyond the last full stop
through the sweating graves
and beyond
far from the dreams and fears of men
through a land without remorse
your feet will keep you walking

where you have strayed
there is no quarter asked for
no prisoner taken
no last-gasp cigarette
not the echo of a prayer
your feet will keep you walking
from the hall to the temple to the isle
to the sanctuary
where a bed of soft flowers
has been prepared
fragrances shared
in the intimate bower

the sword cuts where it
will cut
the flowerhead lies
face up
your lover lies face down
your abnegation knows no bounds

your intestines are held in place
by faith alone
your legs walking you
by faith alone
as you draw near
a ladderless climb

through even the loneliest
of places
the barest of hills, slave-driven cities
mad kings
and wars against babies

you will hardly care
for already you can smell it
the heady incense in the air
the fragrance of her hair

as you light the candle
you'll know
this one flame can tear worlds
obliterate pasts
turn fancy into shame
make a mess out of blame
and dumb lies
and all the bobs and whistles
of a good life well lived

in the end it's the journey itself
that holds you, blindsided
hearing the siren cry
over the horizon
on the other side of the ocean

on the other side of the storm
but close
right in your ear
breathing in your ear
breathing from real lips
hearing the tingling breath
hearing the fall, the tumbling fall
the crying avalanche
of waves on rocks
all that the wisperings entice
and more, for the heart of the ocean
lies with the shore

as you reach for the knife
your hands have lost their tremble
your legs have given up walking
and you are at last
ripe
and ready for the sacrifice

intoxication

make your peace, find your grace
peel your skies back

make moon eyes at the Beloved
embrace the warm ground

slip through the mirror
into a sweet elfin dream

hold hands with your delightful double
travel to impossible galaxies

paint the town red
hum with your own body electric

linger in scented gardens
drink from an overflowing cup

sleep the sleep of sweetness
in the sweetness of sleep

all of these things and more
lie within your compass
and suggest themselves
to the waking mind
the ever-tricksy mind
and the honest heart
most honest heart
never to part

but come home at night
to a light on the porch
some salad, still fresh
a piece of Christmas cake
(no longer fresh)

and a little something left in the bottle

something for the ferryman

pennies fell from heaven
then they didn't

someone else must've needed them

we collected what we could
while we could
those we were able to find
in likely and unlikely places
scurrying about
here, there and everywhere
like blind ants at a picnic

pennies from heaven
heaven's graces

wow! we thought
the lord of all
must have deep pockets
deeper than our hopes
deeper than the world
deeper than love

and we are such greedy little creatures
we always want a little extra
please

oh, we hardly dared
count our blessings
even as we spent them
there were pennies everywhere
falling night and day
out of the generous sky
so who would worry
tomorrow as always
has to take care of itself
and all the other tomorrows
crowding in
are on their own

today is a big enough handful
even with pennies galore
somebody wants more
somebody has less
and we need a few for the cake

it's every man for himself
by the look of things

we took them for granted, I suppose
those passing pennies
we always had our hands in our pockets
a rosy fire in our bellies
and something for the ferryman

then they stopped
the sky was full then it was empty
there were no more pennies
not even for the cake

I guess they were never ours
in the first place
they were passing by
and while one side might have borne
the image of plentitude and
sheaves of corn
the other
was none other
than the face of hunger

the quickening

something always quickens
in the deep
that's what the deep is for

could be love, could be war

with the quickening
comes the awakening
and with the awakening
comes the hunger
and with the hunger
comes the clawing and pawing
the drilling and killing
promise and betrayal

I'm not sure what to do with this
which way to turn
which doors to open and
which to close
and who might already have
come and gone

follow the quickening
consecrate the awakening
feed the hunger

and doors will open and close
by themselves
as if under ghostly influence
landscapes
and possibilities of landscapes
will rush by
like a cascade of prophesies
and all things possible
will be possible

and when that glad day comes
there will once more be the deep
the deep stillness of the deep
where something quickens

it always does

two breaths have I

you have a breath
a dark breath
you have a breath
a light breath

each one to the other
is a reflection
of that which might be
if everything else were
in balance

if everything else were even-stevens
all being equal, one breath
would usher the next
with an easy reciprocity

one's out to the other's in
one's in to the other's out
mist on the mirror

it all comes out in the wash
they say
but I don't know about that
anymore

what should come quite naturally
turns out to be
an exercise in metaphysics
with the dark breath and the light
breath
taking place
way beyond the body
somewhere
with the mirror turned
to face the other way
to the other side of the self
where breath becomes light

you have a body
a dark body
you have a body
a light body

each in love with the other
the other in love with each

most gentle revenge

good friends and comrades
be gentle
with those who hurt you
for they hurt worse

their wound
is double yours

and besides
it's always ten times worse
to be forgiven
than to be accused
so you have the satisfaction
of knowing
that your gentle solicitation
cuts
far deeper
than any knife

she's not what she seems

cultivate the Beloved
at great risk to life and limb
she's not what she seems

however nice it might feel
her lips on yours
her hand on your thigh
the softest part
there's a joker in the deal
a scratch that won't heal
a heart that won't feel
a hand that can't cry

once there was order
order sweet order
sequence and sequins
procession possession succession

then the Beloved comes through the door
everything flies up and about
a big whirly shout
and the ceiling becomes the floor

there's a poltergeist loose
look out
watch for fallout
for the drunken goose
for the lame excuse

and that broken cup
the one your grandmother gave you
from another age
the famous one
can't be glued back together
without the seams showing
to the careful eye

it's just not the same, is it?
best bury it with honours
and real tears
and put your signature
to the memory
before signing off
cultivate the Beloved and you might die
since in death life grows new wings
sprung from painfully human shoulders

and it's hard to know
what you are
let alone what you are becoming

cultivation

allow time for it
give it space, room to grow
to show its face
to come clean, to make amends
put on a show
declare its intentions
colour its petals pink

things do not come forward
of their own accord
but need a little coaxing
a little stroking under the chin
a few sweet nothings
for the shy one, the shyest of all
the veiled one
the whispered one
who parts her flesh
only to the red dawn and no other

until tomorrow
this gift of flowers

try

a little humming at the back of the throat

a light drumming of fingers on stretched skin

a thrumming on the kettledrum

an up-tempo two-step

a platter of memories and a book of hours

allow time for it

to arrive, to be

give it a place and

space

a touch of grace

and there it is

quivering and uncertain

but alive

oh yes, alive

next time around

this time around
you came to it late
so late
leaning to one side
like the walking wounded
like the last bird in the nest
with too much past, not enough future
and a muddled vision

there was a lot going on you didn't know about
you turned your face the other way
hid your eyes
and never once had to think
about the *this* and the *that*
and worlds unseen
the peripheral stink
the paraphernalia of a collision
with the Beloved

coming to, you didn't know
the place
for what it was
or yourself

for what you had once been

after all that forgetting
you couldn't find your bearings
and the compass swung wildly about
in search of directions

your feet didn't know their left
from their right
let alone your mouth find
the right inflections

the rain felt unfamiliar
on your face
and the furnace in your lungs
appeared to come, by the taste of it,
from another planet
where there are creatures who talk
with their skin
paint with scent
and make love with their voices

it took a long time to understand
the *whys*, the *whiches* and *wherefores*
let alone the *neverthelesses*
and the *notwithstandings*

you weren't accustomed
to this sort of treatment
the summary executions
and the bright-edged laughter
the boot through the brain at 3 a.m
the shakes at breakfast

you weren't accustomed to people
who smile on the other side
of their faces
and whose words grow backwards
into their mouths
like eager parasites

where the sun is turned inside out
and men go to work inside their briefcases
and somebody has to pay for everything
except what's owed

you didn't have the stomach
for that sort of thing
and who could blame you
for dragging the chain
and looking about for another
chance

you couldn't hold onto a childhood
that was only in your mind
as if there were some comfort there
some refuge
some sweet ease for the heart
knowing how foolish that is
but being foolish anyway
because folly was all that was left
in the heat of the moment

it's different now
you've caught up
not running behind on little legs
crying 'wait for me!'
you have come home
and seen the place as it always was
but could never be
seen worlds come together and part
seen the fantastic lie down
with the ordinary

little wonder you came to it late
but, you know, late is just in time

this time around

the waiting gate

it had to turn out the way it did
there was no other way
no other shape to make

not because of some destiny
or extraordinary fate
or having to play god's catspaw
but the confluence of events
and energies, hopes and fears
memories
and all the trappings of the self

approach the gate
open the gate
take the gate in your mouth

there are choices galore
but only one you can take
and there comes a time
in the space of a breath
when all roads lead back
to the same place
the same beach

the same stand of trees
the same squally sky
up the garden path
around the pond and
through the gate
the waiting gate
the hidden door
to the other side where there are
no gates, nor fences
nor enclosed spaces, nor
rusty books of law

just the taste of the susceptible air
the unbarred sunlight
and maybe somebody
walking beside you holding your hand
by the fingertips
but you can't see them
feeling as alone as alone could be
crying like a child cries
who can't be seen or heard

the Beloved standing at the threshold
like an orphan

and when you try to close the gate
there is no gate
to close
just a graffiti-covered wall

and you knew, then and there
that it would have to turn out
the way it did

the Beloved rules

I went to the Beloved
full of excuses
and met you there

it was an awkward moment
excuses all around

I had to laugh
the look on your face
your voodoo walk
the sudden terror of the blood

a great unexpectedness
opened up like a water lily
with you the dragonfly
wings iridescent
hovering over the still water

we exchanged politenesses
as many as were needed
then kissed like crazy
because that was the only thing
left to do

you can't script these things
you can't imagine them
you can't believe them
but in the land of the Beloved
the Beloved rules
her face everywhere
on every billboard and bleacher
screen and scene

we knew why we were there
and who was to blame
and where judgement might fall
but what the hell
by the time the kissing was done
and we were getting naked
we ran right out of excuses
though we had plenty to spare

and rose from the dead
feeling the wind in our hair
the blood in our veins
the bubble of words on our lips

and the hand we were
each to each
holding

the gift

on the street mourners gather
the shadow of the mountain
stretches across the plain

a woman waits by a crayon-blue tree
wind picking at her skirt
trying to remember the sky

from her secret hide out
a little girl watches
birds turning into fish
and trees with their hearts on fire
and a sky that unwinds
into the night

a great astonishment of being
you could never have guessed

the girl returns
under a sky of juicy stars
through the shaows of many worlds
to the secret lover of her soul
the crayon woman

who
coils into bed with her
caresses her memories
and whispers into her ear
incantations that bare the body
and saturate the spirit

mourners return to the mountains
the woman returns to the sky
the girl rises into new day

the deserter

I couldn't stand watch for you
during the night
my faith firm, texts memorised
because the night was endless
an endless night
(we couldn't end this night)
the air too cold
and the morning too long ago
to be properly recalled
or accounted for
in this neverending war

I didn't have the heart for it
and started to see things
to smell people long dead
fucking in their graves
their bones crunching together
to hear gargoyles rutting in the shadow
of the eaves of overgrown temples
with the temple whore
and forgot to sing

you stole all the heat
on your quest for the perfect love
the most rapturous, most transcendent
love
to the shivering core
a healing touch
to the soul's own sore

more heat than the body can take
spilling out into the night
the colder-than-hell night
the bogeyman night

I was to stand watch
with prayers at the ready
over this most fragile thing
the spirit of a newborn
about to be wed
to be, and to be more
but at the first hapless cry
and indrawn breath
I turned tail and fled

the transformation

Rumi knows the secret
of the soul's furtive lover
who approaches unbidden
partially hidden
bearing the midnight flame
and a woodland touch

Rumi calls her the Guest
and guest she is
more than a ghost
a midnight flush in red
or a visitation from his head
the Guest walks through the poet's heart
through the heavenly host
and the kingdom of the beast
to sit down at the feast without a blush
calls for wine and dancing
makes a huge fuss
while the gossips all gossip
from behind their hands
and nothing gets said

poets prepare the way
strewing flowers on the bed
and words every which way

with an expectant heart
and labouring breast
hands do a little ballet
on the pillow
where her head will rest

she might come, or she might not
she is like the wind that way
hither and thither
like a dandelion seed

hear her cries
wherever the wind holds sway
glimpsed only
when deep in play
whose laughter fades to gray
when the sun will rise

nothing more than a whisper
on the curtain
as the curtain parts
and the window reveals

the garden and moon-child
in full voice
as the song starts

she is
hidden but not hidden
hidden in plain sight
plain as night
standing before you
the soul's clandestine lover
image of the Beloved

respecting the Guest

when the Guest arrives at the door
make her welcome
give her a hug and offer her
some kitchen clatter
a drink or a little more

the blessings of the house
and some light chatter
if you must

it may be best, my profligate lover,
to think of her
as a messenger from beyond the mind
a manifestation of earth and sky
and all that lies between
seen and unseen
a pagan spirit of a kind
complete with twigs and leaves
and pixie dust

a song from a far star
that fell with a shock

think of her as a tree, a rock,
a quiet stream
rain after a drought
a clear sky above the flood
rising above flesh and blood
and everyday lust

she is upswept and in step
cool and sweet
as fragile as a love lyric
as strong as a prayer
the gold clasp in her hair

she is the Guest

not a manifestation
of the lunar day
or convocation of numbers
or the fevers of Rumi
with his hectic lines
and his heart
breaking apart

but rather
clothed in human flesh
held together

by trembling bones
with a dry mouth
and a thudding pulse

no messenger at all, actually
but from the self
to the self
witnessed in the words
of the poet
who only seeks to give her
the best the house can offer

the nature of the Guest

the Guest comes
only when she is called
when your pleas
resonate with her blood

I have no mouth but I must scream
reads a title from the shelf
among your books of wisdom

that's why the Guest is here
why you find her at the table
or under the rose bush
in the scent of manuka blossom
the twittering of a skylark
or the austere warmth of a lily

in the end there is no escaping her
she has come to give your face its mouth back
to open the voice in your chest
to watch you part your lips

and hear you scream

warm the tea on a gentle flame

it's okay to dread
the arrival of the Guest
the twitch of the curtain
the slip and the flirt

you can't know
exactly what she brings
but that it will shake you
it will break you
even as she sits and sips her tea
adjusts her skirt
and lights up with glee

best make no plans

afterwards
after all that came before
she will take out her lyre
tease its strands
and sing you a refrain
not even Rumi could devise
for it admits no boundaries
but its own dripping notes

of rain and fire
and the secret melodies
of her hands

a song like that
can change you, exchange you
and when you turn to look back
everything you can see
the whole affair
has disappeared, like a gate
that was never there

it's okay to dread
the arrival of the Guest
for there's no predicting
the twist of the lyric
the turn of your heart
or where the galaxy is bound

but there's no getting around it
the Guest will arrive
the Beloved will do the same

you might as well prepare
the saucer and the cup
and warm the tea on a gentle flame

the gardenia

in the inner chambers
with the sound of water slipping
over mossy stones
you remove her veil

it's made of starlight and lace
edged in snowflake
and myth
with a touch of yellow
at the centre
for secret love

this is the moment
this is what you came here for
what has had you on edge
all these years
from the time you first
took the sky into your chest

like a swan you glide over
your disturbing shadow

hiding your eyes away
from petals of deft light
and the sly laughter of girls

whenever you walked into the wild
she was there, a power
so elemental
you didn't know her for what she was
or hear any wedding sounds

when the wild comes into you
a storm on the sky's wing
or in the stillness of green
to rattle your heart
she walks alongside
she opens your past
to show you
its invisible hiding places

how could you not
lead her into the garden
saturated by the scent of gardenias
blinded by their purity
inhale her scent
where the sunlight falls
and the world is quicksilver and dapple

lift her veil of starlight and lace
and see what there is
to be seen

a corolla of elegant white

they're here

tyres crunch on the gravel
the wine teeters
on the rim of the glass
music softly plays
a door opens and closes

in shuttered rooms men decide
the fate of the world
who will live and who will die

indistinct laughter is heard
from the bushes, the rhododendrons
and the chrysanthemums
in the warming air
where the children run and have their fun
wherever the devil may dare

girls and boys come to play
the moon doth shine as bright as day

and out they come, like forest sprites
like a trick of the light
holding hands and cartwheeling

to the effervescent action
of their limbs
free of care
creatures of earth and air

footfalls thud in the hallway
the wind trembles in the glass
music swells
and the voices rise in sweet descant
as the earth tips in its sleep
and all things come to pass

come with a whoop and come with a call come with
good will or not at all

you can hear the children
they come up out of memory
break the surface with a song
and you are ready
ready-steady
as the beast approaches
and the wine spills

as ready as you'll ever be
to join them

up the ladder and down the wall a halfpenny roll
will serve us all

the wooden spoon

Rumi lays out his breakfast
roasted oats, warmed goat's milk
and a dish of honey

he says a quick prayer or two
in case god snatches it all away
before he can lift a spoon

there have been times when
the spoon has left the bowl full
but landed empty on his lips

god can be that quick

once a thief stole the moon from his sky
leaving his window empty for many nights
and a sack of sorrow in his gut

it took a heap of prayers and invocations
to get it back
but the thief had consumed all
but a thin slice
which

with more prayers
and invocations
grew once more into full size
in Rumi's window
large and tasty looking

as he eats, he savours every mouthful
chew for long enough and it all tastes
like god
or tomorrow's grief or joy

he needs all his strength
his humility
he needs his bloodsong
all the magic he can muster
incantations and chants
and age-old prayers

it is said that when he was young
he made birds out of clay
and threw them in the air
where
they turned into real birds
and flew away

but none of that is true
all made up for popular consumption
and to keep his ratings high

the only magic the poet has
lies in his ordinariness
his scuffed slippers, frayed cuffs
his wooden spoon
and the wild beating
of his dervish heart
as he sets out into the day

to meet the Beloved

all that's left

Rumi can barely make it
from the door to the gate
and back again

he can't shake fate
he can't create
his hands won't mend

his skin reeks of the grave
ashes cover his head
tears drip into his wine
ants cover his sheets
dead birds flitter his skies
his lines are inconsolable

his words are gone
all the gold and silver ones
set in their sparkling syntax
glitter
and wink out

all that's left is lies

Beloved, let's fill his cup
lift him from the dead
raise him up
reflesh his bones

let the breath in his chest
move sure and steady
one and another to follow

set him walking

the Guest is coming tomorrow
and Rumi is not ready

the stench

Rumi found something putrid
at the bottom of his garden
something that stank

among the slugs and snails
and maggoty, rotting things
he found something more rank
than nature could devise

a sham
seasoned with deception
wrapped in a lie
that won't break
down
into smaller
bits
because, at the heart of it,
pretense is indivisible
and timeless

Rumi lost his voice
the two sides of his throat

were stuck together
words turned turd

as he bent to take a
closer look
a shadow fell
blotting out the sky
the world turned dark
before his eyes

the wheat, the corn
the leafy greens
and the tiny forget-me-nots
that border the herb patch
and all the slugs and snails
and creeping things
and a sky that flies them all

blotted out
until nothing that was light
was left
except the putrid thing
the false thing
which glowed
like a lump of radioactive
protoplasm

which Rumi tried to bury
with his bare hands and his bare words
in the empty dark

meeting Rumi at the crossroads

at the crossroads
many tracks
led off
to many worlds
true and fake
and multiplying pathways
I could take

to cultivate friends
avoid enemies
and get in good with god

I found a venerable ancient
dressed in Sufi robes
with eyes that veered apart
one to the light, one to the dark

in some other world his double
was busy dancing
to the whirl of his robes
and the thunder of drums

I wasn't going to stop
he's the sort of person you'd
sneak past
in case he reads you a fortune cookie
the worst of fates
but I wasn't to be let off that fast

you want to know which road to take
he said
no, I said, I had my pride
everywhere I went it was by my side

he shook his head
'there are no crossroads,' he said

was this my fortune cookie
my inescapable fate?

'there are no decisions to make
there is only one road to take
all you have to do is walk it'

I waited for the crossroads to vanish
and my road to show itself
that I may walk it
and in that time of waiting

the venerable ancient
wrote many poems, lifetimes of lines
in many worlds, and many histories
and became famous and much studied
by all the universities
in the multiverse
and finally died with honour
or an unmarked grave

the crossroads didn't magically vanish
but I didn't want
to hang around the spooky old wizard
with his veering eyes

the only road
was the one I was walking
so I kept putting one foot
in front of the other
always my best foot forward
sure and steady

'You see', the poet said,
'it is the road that walks

a creature who walks unseen among us

on the road
I died
and had to come back to life
again
all by myself
to walk amongst you

I had to reassemble
my wits
out of all the floating bits
and the flying bits
and the dying bits
and the rumbling, grinding bits
and the bits that didn't fit
the other bits

it was hard work
constructing myself
into a form recognisable
that would pass among the people
as the up and walking
up and talking

real thing
I didn't see a tunnel, or light
to guide my path
or friends waiting to usher me
into the great unknown
rather the steady chant of the poet
reciting the sacred syllables
the many names of god
echoing through the dimensions
that lie
between the land of the living
and the land of the hopeful

I could sing along
after a fashion
as the words were new
fresh as spring
bright as a cornfield
hot as a passion

now I walk
under different stars
made
for an unfamiliar sky
in quite another place
but no matter

what really counts is
that I am alive
after having died

and maybe not for the first time

staying awake

Rumi is tired
from all this quivering
and shivering
quaking and shaking
spasms of fire
and wants to lie down
and sleep
the sleep of the newly born

even a wooden pillow
and iron blankets
feel soft
in the body of sleep
a satiny oblivion
in the deep place beyond space
beyond even the shadow
of desire

but he is fast learning
the price he has to pay
for fleshing himself in the world
as he did, quite recklessly
for being a human being

in the human-created world
and suffering all the ills
the flesh is heir to
even as the world is stolen away

he lights up like a filament
electrified from head to toe
too weary to dance and half in trance
he's made sick
with love

it seems he has understood
too late
what happens after all this courting
and hectic pursuit of the Beloved
who after all
may not wish to be seen
and may try to hide inside a face
only to be discovered
in the deepest recesses of
wakefulness

try something new

if you feel your heart
is about to burst out of your chest
in a spray of blood and foam
and palpitating muscle

maybe it will
maybe that time has come
maybe it's the right thing

if you feel you'll die on the spot
from the touch of love
and the trees and the tangle
of the moon in the trees
and waves of sourceless pleasure

maybe you will
maybe that time has come
maybe it's the right thing

if you feel as if your lungs
are about to cave in
to let in the cold, airless void

between huddles of stars
where there's nothing but god to breathe

maybe they will
maybe that time has come
maybe it's the right thing

if you feel that your legs
are about to give out
and you'll fall over on the street
or while taking a pee
maybe they will
maybe they already have
maybe you're already crawling
towards that ever more distant
horizon
that's rushing towards you
away from you
and you can only propel yourself
forward
on your elbows
when even your knees have given out

or pull yourself along
by the willpower of your fingers alone

until there's nothing left
to get a hold upon

then maybe all that
has already happened
heart lungs and muddy blood
and all the things death feels like

so on the count of three
as in one-two-three
I want you to feel something

altogether quite different

call up the spirits

wind slamming
lightning makes a play
swelling oceans
of blood and guts
stars like skin piercings
nights like death

and the news, the news, the news
is never good

the moon
the Guest, the Beloved
always disappearing
only to creep back up
among the feathery grasses
and mottled shades of the garden

the silky scent of red clover
heady oreganum steeped in the past
thyme that whistles at love

all dressed up with nowhere to go

the ancestors come crowding around
with their desperate histories
their hands breaking open
their eyes in chains
crying out for justice
for flesh, for pleasure
for redress
for well-earned oblivion

you have a children's rhyme
stuck in your throat, a chant
half born
a name that doesn't stick
an angel with folded wings
a passion too big for its boots
you are ready to run
ready to cry

and you can't shut your ears
to the mocking sound of children
the shame and disgrace
and choked up tears

sticks and stones
will break your bones
but names
will never hurt you

sensual senses

that smell of cinnamon spice
like the smell of wool burning
rich and oily

the chirp of the nightingale
is like a distant call
from a morning that comes too early

the smell of the earth
and the moist decay of the ponga fronds
is like the damp on your thighs

the touch of the cardamon night
on your bare skin
has its own intimacy

the way the flowers taste your tongue
is enough to set the garden alight
with a late sunset

and the sight of all you can't see
comes as a revelation
just on time

feeding time

the hunter hunts
the prey has choices
one is to the other
matched
so they tell us

the killing and the willing
but there are shades
of blood and heat
of willing meat
and shades of honest doubt
against the black and the white
and the red
amid the spunk and gore
to come

the hunter may talk to his prey
quite soothingly
and strike when the time is right

the prey may run or demure
or fight, or unveil their hearts
or limp, or play victim

the sweet surrender
the most playful sacrifice
the enticement and rejection
the heartbreak and final squeal
of resignation
as the hunter strikes

and something gets to feed
in the feeding night

make a run for it, friend

when the Beloved comes along
better hide your face
or make a run for it
scatter to the four winds
while there's still time
and a rhyme or two remains

she takes no prisoners
and can slay you with her eyes alone
a mere glance
right and left, men and women
and all those in between
fall over backwards, unbelieving

when she walks the street
fixtures become unfixed
lampposts float sideways
on their pools of sodium light
parking meters joust
shop mannequins seduce customers
with porcelain words
money bursts into flame in pockets
and cash registers

the coffee sits on top of the cream
and there's blood on the ground
from all the hearts that have jumped
right out of their time
and eyes everywhere you look
from those who have torn them out
to hang on trees like rotting fruit
until the trees go blind

it can get that bad, dear friend

terror
and evil visions to the gatekeepers
and the midnight horrors to
the devisers of laws and regulations
the *delirium tremens* to the sober
infinities to the mathematicians
and abstractions to the physicist

everywhere she goes
she'll piss on the pompous
puke on the puritan, mangle marriages
blur boundaries
tap on windows, rap on doors
hide up the street
vanish into forests of flame

lie beside you at night

with her breath upon you
and before you know it
put her hand right through your flesh
to put a little squeeze on your heart
just to remind you

and you, fool,
who forgot to run and failed to hide
have hardly known
a more
blissful ride

cutting up shadows into syllables

Rumi stays at home
making syllables out of the darkness
and, like blowing kisses,
sends them off into the night
into the care of the vagrant winds

he keeps thinking he has
better things to do
but can't think of what
at that moment

everybody is out having fun
dancing and whooping it up
embracing the moonlight
before dawn catches them out

but the lovesick Rumi
is not among them

rather
summoned from the forests of night
to mutter under his breath

frown at the shadows
and wonder how the moon
could get off scot-free
he remains home in chains
amid the wreckage left behind
by a visit from the Beloved

now look at him, scribbling words
like little paper birds
cutting up shadows into syllables
and, like blowing kisses,
sending them off into the imperfect night

star jumper

Rumi dreamed he became a frog
leaping from star to star
without raising a sweat

and breaking the shimmering surface
of spacetime
with his bulbous eyes wide

he isn't the only one
the whole cosmos is filled
with hopping frogs

frogs that hop in
from other universes
even unhopping frogs
that leap backwards
in time

he wakes full of regrets
for being a man
with toenails and underpants
all that baggage
and a dusty walk home

he can't even call himself a tadpole
with a shred of self-respect

no cosmos leaping for him
he can barely hop from the bed
to the door and from the door
to the gate

it's all one foot in front of the other
while one gets left behind
to drag up the rear

a far cry from star-leaping frogs
and a menagerie of other transformations
of which the poet can only dream

stones that turn into birds
as they skip across the inverted pond
of the sky
and the chitter of the skylark
turning into the music of the spheres
and the invention of galaxies
that turn constellations into
ripe fruit

all of these things
and the cartwheeling music

are one and the same as Rumi himself
if he only could see

he is the frog
his mind is the lily pad
and all he has to do is leap about

little wonder being a man
hardly cuts the mustard
nice as it is to have warm blood
and quickening affections

his life is like a turntable turning
in one direction
playing one song only
following as predictably
as lunch follows breakfast

and he finds himself sinking
sinking into the mire
into the mirror
for he has forgotten how to leap
how to break the shimmering surface
breathe
and to set his sights
on the next star

the grand master of regrets

I have no regrets, I said to Rumi
but he didn't believe it
he's heard it all before
and said the same thing himself
on many occasions

it's the sort of thing people say
when things aren't looking too good

to regret is to be human, he said
but it sounded far too pompous
as if he were trying to be Confucius
instead of the poet with twigs
in his hair
large froggy feet
a few leftover phrases
from the dance of the god-driven

and so many goddamn regrets
he's lost count

along with faces and names
and missed opportunities

and stolen eternities
and days lost to the silly business
of having to be human
and keep up appearances
wearing clothes, eating all the time
nodding and smiling, pissing, preening
and pretending

you could say that Rumi
is the grand master of regrets
which is why
I've gotta have them too
you see
because he couldn't be alone
in something like that
suffering is isotropic
and the broken-hearted
never believe in love

I'm not so sure
I leave my regrets at the door
and forget to collect them
when I leave

a little trick I picked up
from Rumi in his better days

when he knew how to leave stuff behind
and never had to cross the same river
twice

but the poor poet has forgotten
how to laugh
and can't bear the thought of it

I try to get him on a jolly trolly, but you
know how it is with the broken-hearted
all he wants to do is drink
and talk to the moon

most of us have better things to do

time kills

you have to pause a while
to feel the full weight of this

you have to give it
due consideration

the sun that rose brightly
sinks into a murky haze

the heart that started out so eager
begins to labour

and (take a deep breath)

a thought you could once live with
becomes unsupportable

they say you have a receptive heart
but you know the moment
when it turned to iron
and what was okay
sort of
was not okay anymore
ever

you have to pause a while
for the reality of it all
to sink in
and oh how far it sinks!

now you can join Rumi
in his happy hell
and let him know the bad news

no getting off the hook

the scary part is
that there is no fate
to fate us
or destiny
to destiny us
or even god to god us

or fix us in some stupid future
among a host of futures

there's just us and us
and all that we pretend

the scary part is
that we are required to act
to move our mouths
and not have some other agency
move them for us

to pick up this and let go that
in good time and without losing
balance

to make something different
a little less stupid
and a little more to the point
we might just out-fate fate
leave destiny in the dust
and god on the hook
while we get on with it

the empty boat

Rumi knows what it's like
to slip like an empty boat
over still water
and be a host to grief
while bravely working

he knows what it's like
to empty the house
for the arrival of the Guest
and make paper chains
for the festivities
even as he plans his exit

he knows how it feels
to bite back tears
and fears
when contemplating the horrendous
state of the world
in its holocaust of madness

he knows that lovers are sleepless
because they feel the secret solitude
of the Beloved all around them

Rumi knows what it's like
to have his words fall flat
just like that
no taking them back
Jack
they're already done
rare, medium, burnt to a crisp

he knows what it's like
to be a cow that flies
or a goat that barks
or a chicken that never
comes home to roost

all of these things he knows
and other things
too wild to relate
because we'd have to draw
oceans above the sky
and make decent intervals
indecent
until we hardly knew our stops
from our starts
+

better to leave him in his empty boat
in his boatlessness in his tearlessness
in his wordlessness
in his indecency and his
secret solitude

and be on our way

if just for once

the urge to do something new
got Rumi off his backside
putting on a new coat
and opening some new doors
walking some new streets
breathing some fresh air
spitting out some old words
and generally seeing the world
in a novel way

he'd had enough of the same old
same old it was time to blow things wide apart
with a kiss
or something a little stronger

it was time to vanish into an ant's head
in front of a vast crowd
of screaming fans
or turn into a brightly plumed
bird of wonder
at a poetry convention
and fly off into the sun
in lyrical grandeur
a final gesture to time and circumstance

in short, here was an opportunity
amid the wreckage
to quit fooling around with heartbreak
and mooning over the Beloved
to pull up his socks
tie his shoelaces in a neat bow
and turn a corner before it disappears

everything and anything is possible
he wouldn't want his face to fix
in any particular grimace
in case the wind changed
and the grimace stayed forever

he wouldn't want to stick with
some style of walking
like a prisoner in chains
or find himself laughing at stale jokes
in a stale house
where it's either too early or too late
or any other unthinkable fate

let his face be an open book
let his love-struck eyes tell all
to all who tell
let his hands open and shut like sea anemones

feel the shiver of twilight at noon
hear the ancestors' distant cry
feel the ocean large and round
between his palms

let him cross some new bridges
make some new mistakes

and let him go

body up

Rumi went to see god
who came to earth as the Guest
who is the ever-changing face
of the Beloved
and is the mother of all verse

and said, 'hey you, whatever-your-name
you who sit in judgement on mere mortals
and other lowly creatures
haven't you heard what the poet said
bodied, one will hunger
bodied, one will lie

if you don't know about this
or have forgotten
then try it for yourself
get yourself a body just like mine
flesh and bone, blood and guts

and see how you like it

Also by Mike Johnson

Novels
Driftdead
Lethal Dose
Zombie in a Spacesuit
Hold My Teeth While I Teach You to Dance
Travesty
Counterpart
Stench
Dumbshow
Antibody Positive
Lear: The Shakespeare Company Plays Lear at Babylon

Shorter Fiction
Confessions of a Cockroach/Headstone
Back in the Day: Tales of NZ's Own Paradise Island
Foreigners

Poetry
Ladder With No Rungs, Illustrated by Leila Lees
Two Lines and a Garden, Illustrated by Leila Lees
To Beatrice: Where We Crossed the Line
Vertical Harp: The Selected Poems of Li He
Treasure Hunt
Standing Wave

From a Woman in Mt Eden Prison & Drawing

Lessons

The Palanquin Ropes

Non-Fiction
Angel of Compassion

Children's Fiction
Kenni and the Roof Slide, Illustrated by Jennifer
Rackham
Taniwha. Illustrated by Jennifer Rackham

CPSIA information can be obtained
at www.ICGtesting.com
Printed in the USA
LVHW030248270121
677549LV00012B/2425

9 780995 128293